How To Draw
DONKEY KONG™
& Friends

Written by Michael Teitelbaum

How-To-Draw Art by Leif Peng

Troll

A Creative Media Applications Production

Written by Michael Teitelbaum

How-To-Draw Art by Leif Peng

Art Direction by Fabia Wargin Design

Hello there, video game fans and future artists.

Cranky Kong here. My grandson, Donkey Kong (I know you've heard of him), was too lazy to write the introduction to this book himself. As usual, he asked me to step in and save his hairy hide. So here I am to welcome you to this "How to Draw" book. Put down your Nintendo game machine for a little while (don't worry, you can pick it up later) and take a journey from the fancy, colorful, high-tech world of Donkey Kong Country to the wonderful low-tech world of paper and pencils.

All great ideas (such as the "Donkey Kong Country" video game) start off on the drawing board. A couple of lines and circles can become a well-loved character—like me! With this book, you'll learn to draw all the Kongs, as well as their friends and enemies.

This book will take you, step-by-step, through the process of drawing the characters that live in that jolly jungle known as Donkey Kong Country. You'll start out with some circles and lines. Later, you'll add the details that give each character his or her own look.

Practice each of the characters until you feel comfortable drawing him or her. Then put your imagination to work. Start thinking of situations and stories to put us into. You can do a comic strip, a storybook, or even a giant-sized poster of your favorite Kongs and Kremlings.

So, enough talk already. I'm a monkey of action! Pick up your pencils and get ready for some cartooning fun. **Here are a few tips before you begin:**

1) Draw lightly as you sketch. You'll have plenty of time to darken your lines as you finish your drawing and fill in the details.

2) Stay loose! Let your hand and arm move freely. Don't grip your pencil like you're trying to choke a Kremling! Drawing should be fun and relaxing.

3) Don't be afraid to make a mistake—that's why erasers were invented!

4) Remember, the poses in this book are guides to help you understand the shapes that make up Donkey Kong and the rest of the good guys and bad guys. As you practice (and you must practice if you are going to improve), you'll soon be able to create your own poses, situations, and stories. But be patient! It takes time to get comfortable drawing.

So turn the page and get started. Oh, one last thing. Do me a favor. When you draw Donkey and Diddy, please try to get them to listen to me and my vast experience a bit more. I'll really appreciate it.

Happy drawing!

Donkey Kong's Head

Let's start off with a front view of Donkey Kong's head:

1

Begin by drawing two equal-sized circles. Stack them so that they overlap by about 1/3 of their height. Then draw the one vertical and two horizontal "guide lines," as shown.

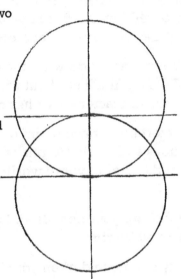

2

Add the eyebrows, eyes, nostrils, and mouth along the center vertical line.

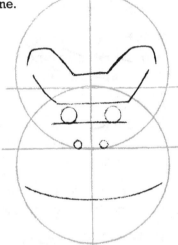

3

Next add the ears, hair, jaw, and other details, as shown.

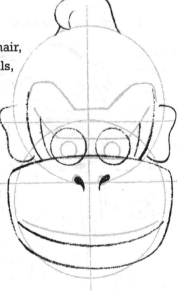

4

Erase the guide lines, and you've got Donkey Kong in all his gorilla glory!

Donkey Kong's Expressions

Now that you've practiced a straight-on view of Donkey Kong, let's turn him a little to the side and give him some expression. You'll still begin with two stacked circles. But to turn his head, you must turn and curve the guide lines, as shown.

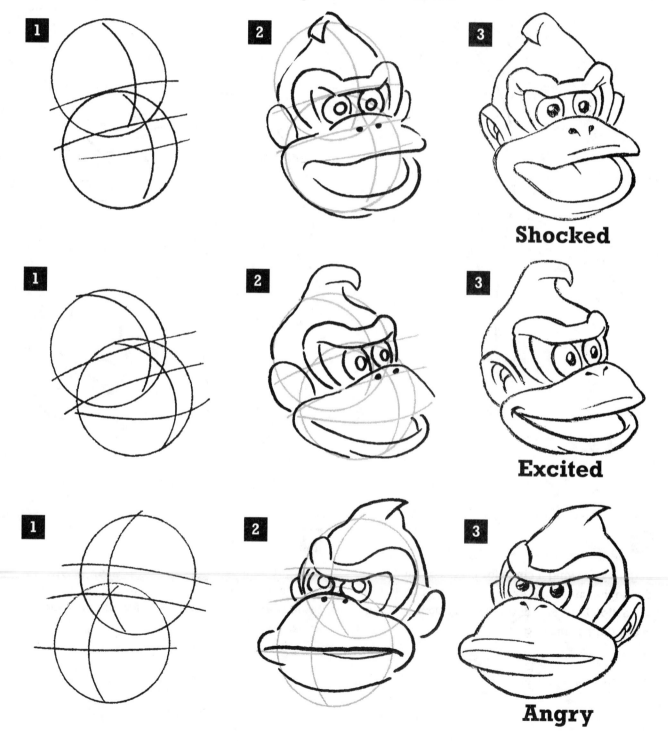

Shocked

Excited

Angry

Donkey Kong's Body

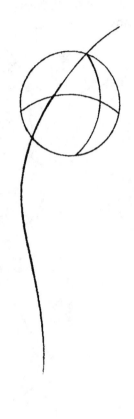

1

Begin by drawing a circle for his head. Then divide the circle into four quarters, as shown. Add an "action line" to indicate the way Donkey Kong is standing or moving.

2

Map out Donkey Kong's chest, arms, and legs using circles, as shown. Note how the circles for his legs are smaller that those for his chest and arms.

Everyone needs a good head on his shoulders, and Donkey Kong is no exception. Once you've practiced DK's head and facial expressions, you're ready to move on to drawing his whole body:

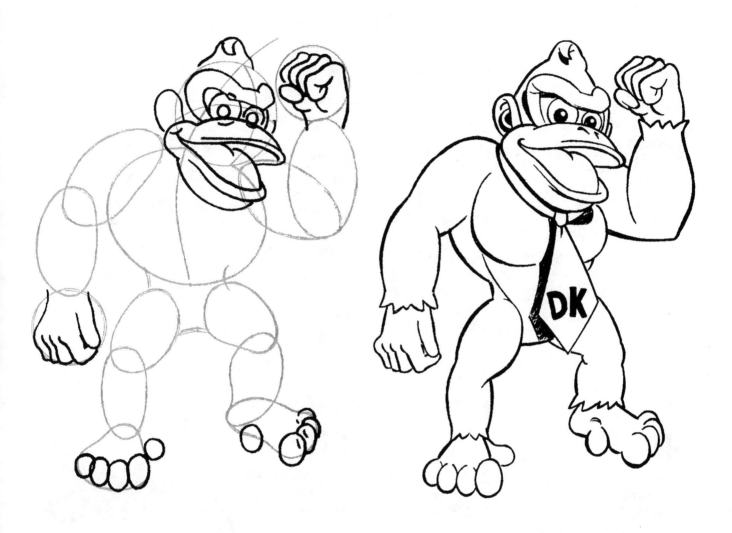

3

Next add the facial details (see page 4), the hands, and the toes.

4

Join the circles, as shown. Then add the final details, such as DK's tie and his "cuffs" (on both his wrists and his ankles). Erase the construction lines, and that's it! Congratulations! You've just completed your first full-figure Donkey Kong drawing. Don't worry if it's not perfect. You've just taken a big step toward illustrating your own DK adventures. Keep practicing!

Diddy Kong's Head

Most stories have more than one character, so let's move on to drawing Donkey Kong's little buddy, Diddy Kong:

1 Start out with the same circles and guide lines that you used for Donkey Kong.

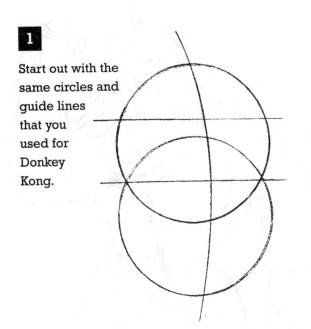

2 However, Diddy's eyes are much larger than those of his big buddy. Draw them as shown. Then add his cap and his mouth.

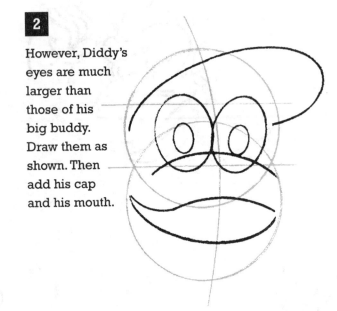

3 Add Diddy's ears and the other detail lines shown here.

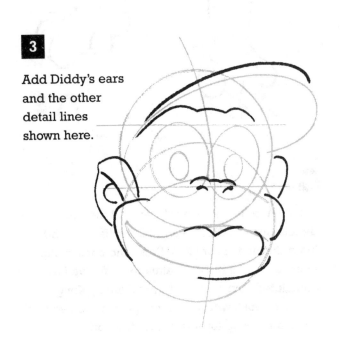

4 Finish up by erasing your construction lines. Then add shading, as shown, around Diddy's eyes, eyebrows, and ears, and on the bottom of the cap's bill. Now you've drawn Diddy in all his simian splendor!

Diddy Kong's Expressions

Once again, we turn the head a bit and work on some expression. Use the two curved horizontal guide lines to set the distance between Diddy's nostrils (which rest on the lower line) and the top of his eyes (which end at the upper line). Now practice the details of these three expressions:

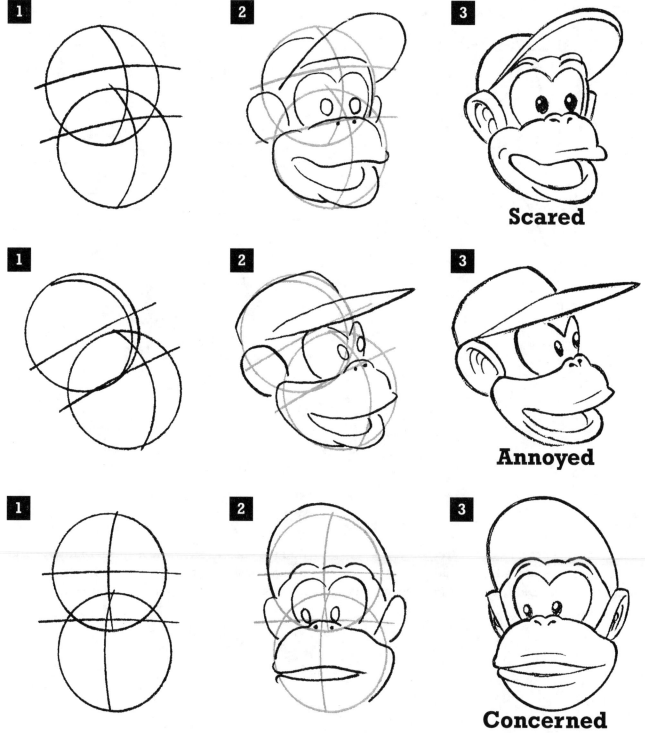

Scared

Annoyed

Concerned

Diddy Kong's Body

1

Begin with the basic head construction you've already learned, and add the action line to indicate the way Diddy is standing (or leaning, in this case).

2

Add the lines, as shown, to map out Diddy's short, round body, arms, and legs. Unlike Donkey Kong, Diddy's arms and legs are about the same size.

Now let's get Diddy up on his feet:

3

Start filling in the details on his head (see page 8), hands, and feet. Don't forget his cap.

4

Add the final touches, as shown, and Diddy is ready to join the cast of characters in your original Donkey Kong adventures.

Dixie's Body

1

Begin with the basic head construction and action line.

2

Add lines, as shown, for Dixie Kong's body, hat, arms, legs, and—of course—her famous ponytail. Note that Dixie Kong's body is similar to Diddy's, but it's a little more peanut-shaped.

Wherever Diddy goes, his friend Dixie Kong is sure to follow and help him on his quest. Let's add her to the list of characters you can draw:

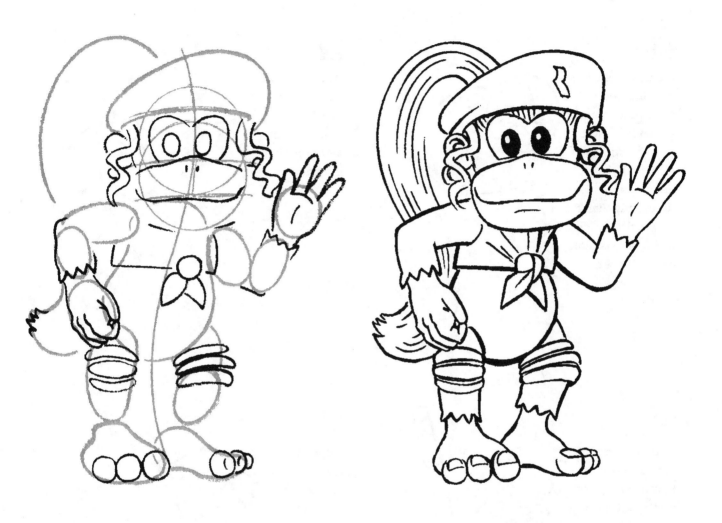

3

Start to fill in the details, such as fingers, toes, costume, and face.

4

Don't forget Dixie Kong's kneepads and the details on her powerful ponytail.

Cranky Kong

No Donkey Kong adventure would be complete without DK's grousing granddad, Cranky Kong:

1

Begin, as usual, with the head construction and action line. Note how the circles for Cranky's head line up differently than the others do, and that his action line is more stooped over.

2

Add details, as shown. Note that Cranky's legs are thin and bend in at the knees.

3

Add facial details, hands, feet, beard, cane, and eyeglasses.

4

Put in the finishing touches on Cranky's hair, cuffs, and

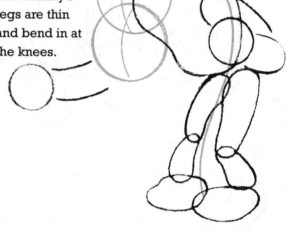

sleeves. You can almost hear Cranky complaining!

Funky Kong

He's the coolest dude ever to fly a plane. He's Funky Kong, and here's how to draw him:

1

Funky's body proportions are the same as Donkey Kong's. Start off with the head circles and action line.

2

Add the body, arm, and leg ovals, which are similar to those of Donkey Kong.

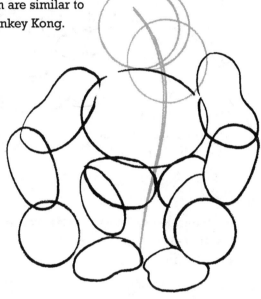

3

Now add the details: sandals, sunglasses, kerchief cap, and neck chain and medallion. Here is where Funky really begins to look like himself.

4

Put in the finishing touches, as shown, and you've completed the final member of the Kong clan!

Rambi the Rhino

The Kongs have lots of friends—and enemies. Let's learn how to draw some of them, starting off with their friend Rambi:

1

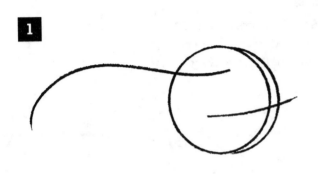

First draw Rambi's head circles. Notice that they are very close together and that the action line is horizontal.

2

Add the body and leg shapes, keeping in mind that Rambi's head is very large in proportion to the rest of his body.

3

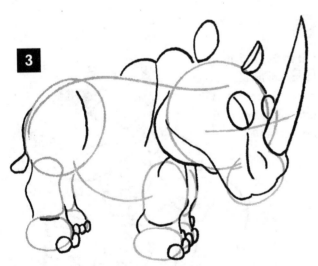

Add the two bumps on his back, the horn on his nose, his toes, and the basic shapes for his eyes, ears, and tail.

4

Fill in the remaining details—eyes, tail, and mouth—and you've got Rambi to add to your Kong quests.

Expresso the Ostrich

Expresso is a speedster and a good friend of the Kongs:

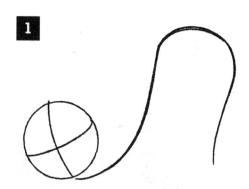

1

Start off with a single circle for Expresso's head. Divide this into quarters, as shown. Then draw a large curve to serve as your action line for Expresso's body.

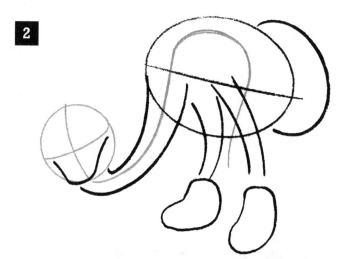

2

Add shapes for the body, back feathers, legs, shoes, and beak.

3

Fill in the facial details, feathers, and shoes. Notice the bumps on Expresso's feathers and his knobby knees, which bend backward.

4

Fill in the remaining details, as shown, and you're done!

Enguarde the Swordfish

Enguarde has helped out the Kongs on their sea adventures. Here's how to draw him:

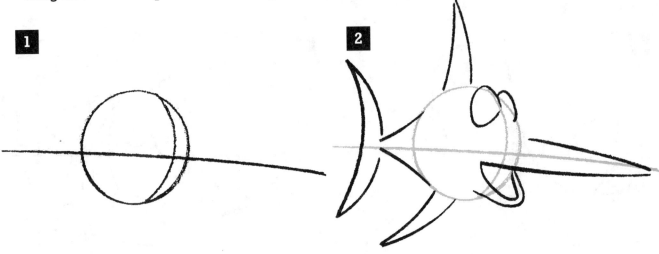

1 With most of the characters in this book, the action line for the pose extends down from the head. Enguarde's action line travels right through the middle of a single circle used for his head and body. Add a curve inside the circle to help position his eyes.

2 Fins, tail, and swordlike snout are all long, thin, triangular shapes that extend out from the body circle. Draw these in now. Notice that the eyes sit in the top quarter of the head.

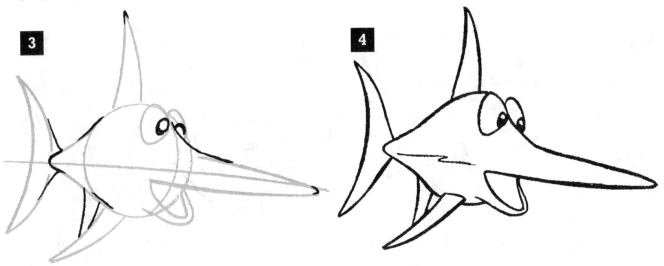

3 Fill in his pupils, and add the fin that hangs below Enguarde's body. Then join his body parts with smooth, sweeping curves.

4 Smooth out the details, as shown, then add a "lightning bolt" stripe along his side. Now Enguarde's ready to join the Kongs for some undersea action!

Squawks the Parrot

Before we finish with the Kongs and their friends, let's draw Squawks. Squawks has lent them a hand (a wing, actually) on many of their adventures:

1

Start with a small circle, but don't let it fool you. Squawks actually has a very large head.

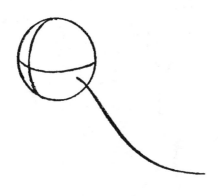

2

Now draw his beak! See what we mean? Add the large body circle, wings, and feet.

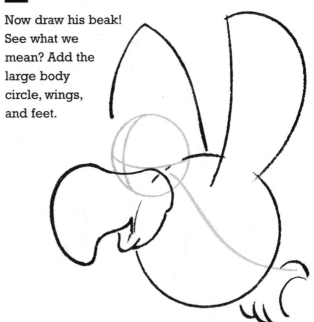

3

Start adding the ruffles on his feathers. Note how the pupils of his eyes sit on the horizontal center line.

4

Fill in the final details, and you're ready to send the Kongs and their friends out on an adventure. But what about the bad guys, you say? We thought you'd never ask!

King K. Rool

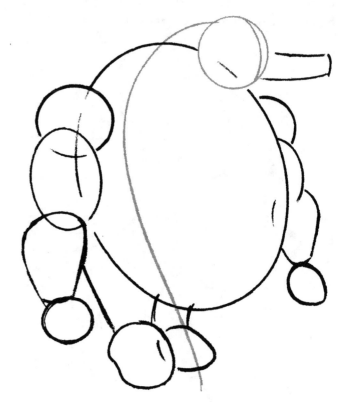

1

As with the good guys, start off Rool by drawing a small circle for his head and an action line. You can see from the placement of the circle on the action line how far forward K. Rool's tiny head sits on his huge body.

2

Add a large oval for this bad guy's big bod, plus smaller ovals to define his arms and legs. Notice how long his arms are. They reach down almost to his feet. Add a rectangle to indicate his jaw.

Now let's learn to draw some of the Kongs' enemies. Let's start off with the baddest of all baddies. Yes, we're talking about King K. Rool, leader of the evil Kremlings:

3

Draw another rectangle on top of Rool's head. Divide it in half horizontally. You'll use the upper half for the spikes on his crown.

4

Add Rool's armbands, cape, and spikes. Finish up the details, as shown, and you're ready to introduce the meanest of all the banana-thieving Kremlings to your original stories and artwork.

Kritter

Kritter is a very typical Kremling. Once you can draw Kritter, you can use his basic form to make up your own Kremlings:

1

Once again, start off with the divided circle and action line.

2

Kritter's body is not as big as King K. Rool's. Draw a circle for the body, then add the additional arm, leg, neck, and jaw shapes, as shown.

3

Next add Kritter's tail, eyes, teeth, fingers, toes, and shoulder armor.

4

Finish the details, as shown, and you've got yourself one regulation-type Kremling.

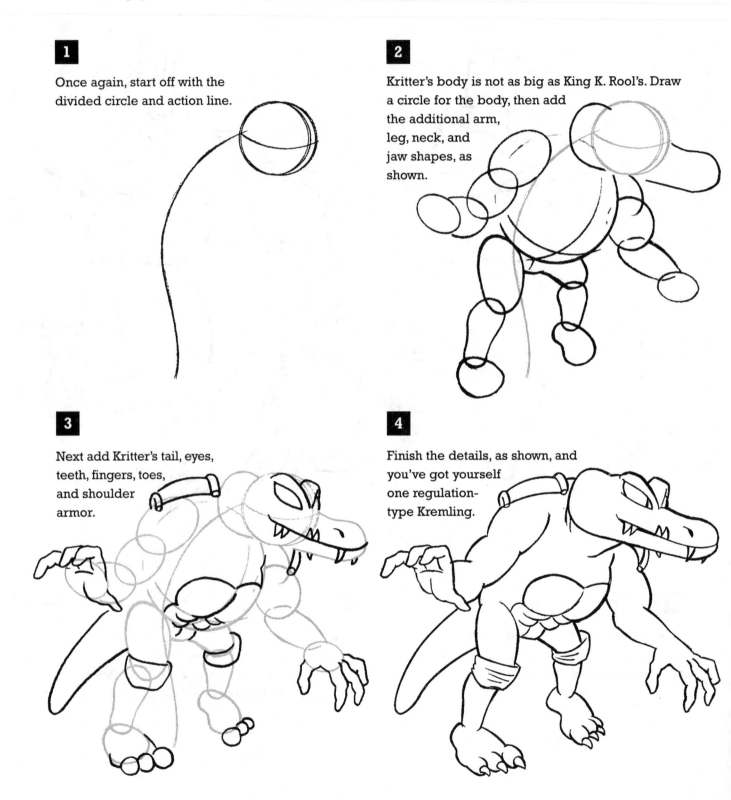

Krusha

Big on muscles but small on brains (don't worry, you don't have to draw those!), Krusha is our next subject:

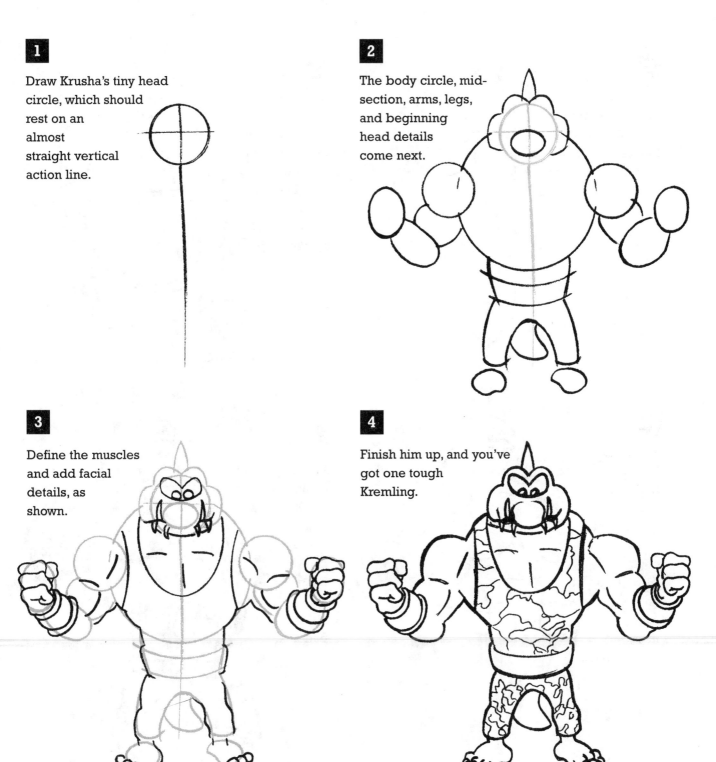

1

Draw Krusha's tiny head circle, which should rest on an almost straight vertical action line.

2

The body circle, mid-section, arms, legs, and beginning head details come next.

3

Define the muscles and add facial details, as shown.

4

Finish him up, and you've got one tough Kremling.

Klump

Klump's big belly and helmet are his most distinguishing features.
Here's how to draw this overfed Kremling:

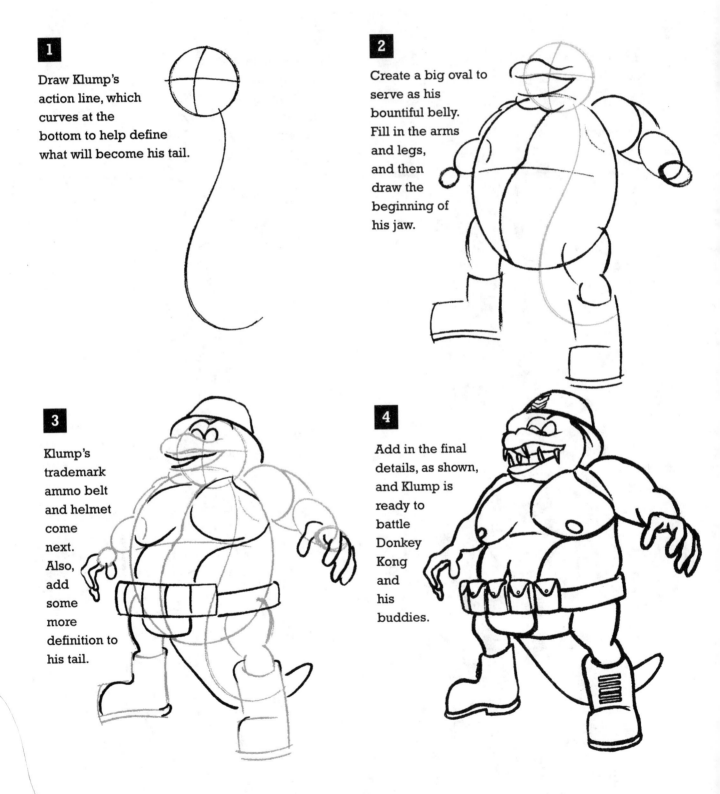

1 Draw Klump's action line, which curves at the bottom to help define what will become his tail.

2 Create a big oval to serve as his bountiful belly. Fill in the arms and legs, and then draw the beginning of his jaw.

3 Klump's trademark ammo belt and helmet come next. Also, add some more definition to his tail.

4 Add in the final details, as shown, and Klump is ready to battle Donkey Kong and his buddies.

Klap Trap

Unlike the Kremlings you've drawn so far,
Klap Trap crawls around on all fours, like a dog:

1

Start off with a fairly large head circle and a
horizontal action line.

2

Give Klap Trap a tiny body but really big jaws. He
didn't get his name for nothing!

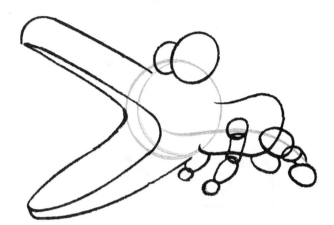

3

Add the teeth, eyes, fingers, toes, and tail.

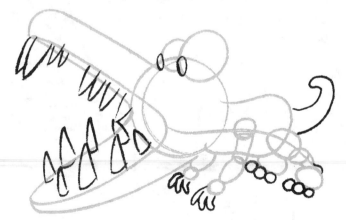

4

His body pattern completes the drawing!

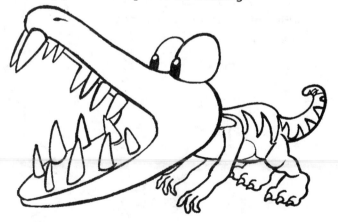

Necky the Vulture

Aerial attacks are a constant threat from this high-flying foe.
Here's how to add him to your collection:

1

Begin with the head circle. The action line, which curves up to indicate the arch of the body, bends down at the end to show where his feet go.

2

Add the beak, eyes, neck, body oval, wings, and feet shapes, as shown.

3

Next come the ruffles on the edges of Necky's wing feathers, plus some additional detail on his feet, neck, beak, and eyes.

4

Add the finishing touches, as shown. Notice how one of Necky's legs is hidden by his body. Just draw one or two toes peeking out.

Zinger

Beware Zinger's stinger and the striking spikes on his back:

1

Zinger's head circle is large, and his action line curves down below him. This will allow you to draw him in attack position, swooping down, stinger first!

2

Add the eyes—which take up the top 2/3 of his head—the body, the stinger, and the wings.

3

Add Stinger's legs, body spikes, and antennae.

4

Add the final details, as shown. Then run for cover!

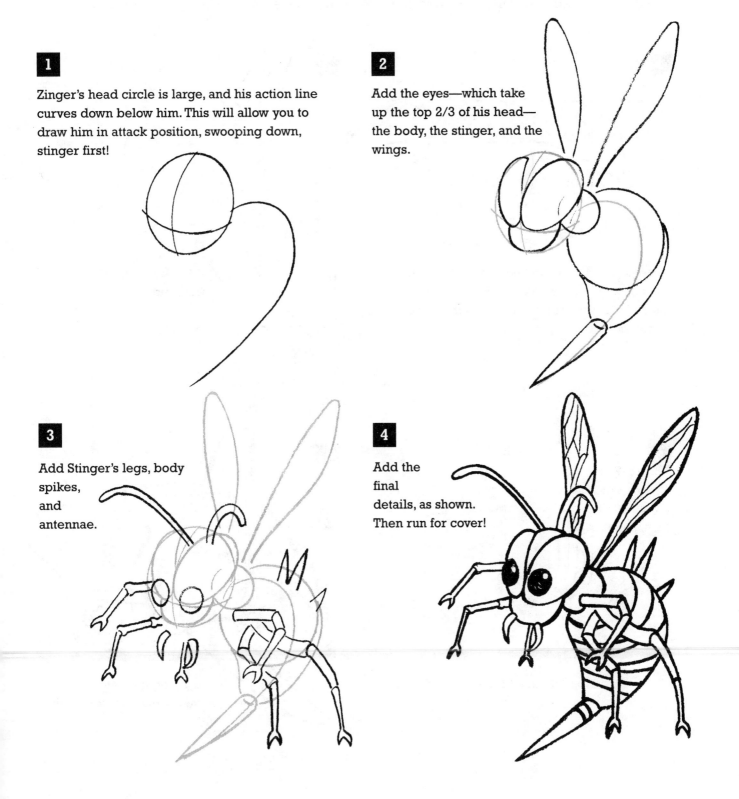

Chomps the Shark

Chomps, one of the Kongs' most dangerous underwater enemies, is different from any of the other characters you've learned to draw so far. Here's a good way to draw him:

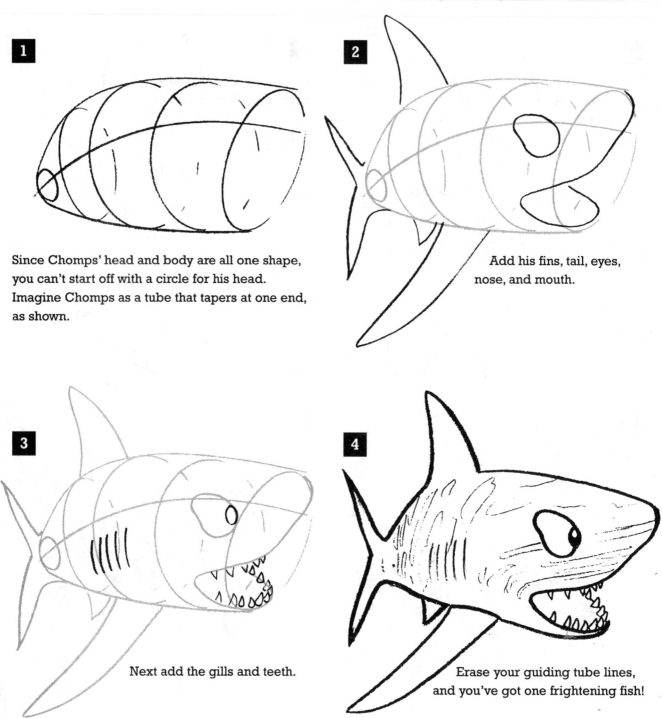

1

Since Chomps' head and body are all one shape, you can't start off with a circle for his head. Imagine Chomps as a tube that tapers at one end, as shown.

2

Add his fins, tail, eyes, nose, and mouth.

3

Next add the gills and teeth.

4

Erase your guiding tube lines, and you've got one frightening fish!

Slippa the Snake

This scaly, slithering enemy also has a unique shape:

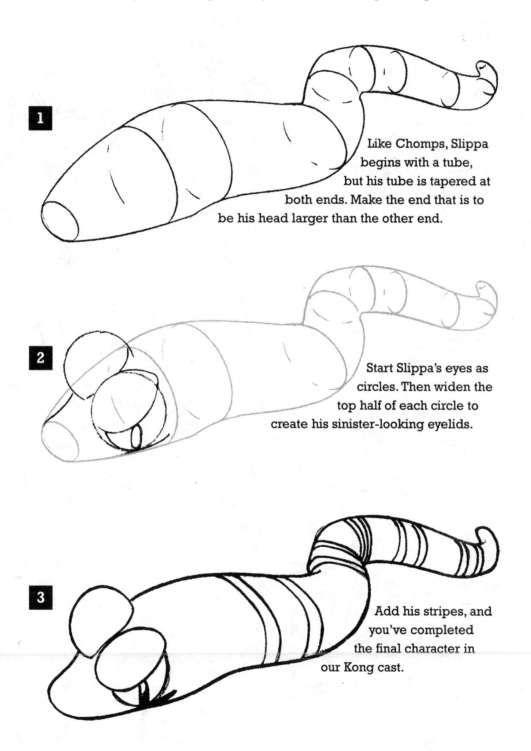

1

Like Chomps, Slippa
begins with a tube,
but his tube is tapered at
both ends. Make the end that is to
be his head larger than the other end.

2

Start Slippa's eyes as
circles. Then widen the
top half of each circle to
create his sinister-looking eyelids.

3

Add his stripes, and
you've completed
the final character in
our Kong cast.

Scenery and Props

• Funky's Plane

• One Type of Donkey Kong Island Palm Tree

• Mining Cart

• Krazy Kremland Roller Coaster Kart

• Exploding Barrel

• DK Barrel

• Kannon Ball and Kannon

Any scene or story that you draw needs to be set somewhere. Here is some scenery to add to your drawing. You will also need to be able to draw some props—objects (such as barrels)—used by the characters in your story. Practice tracing these first, then try drawing them on your own:

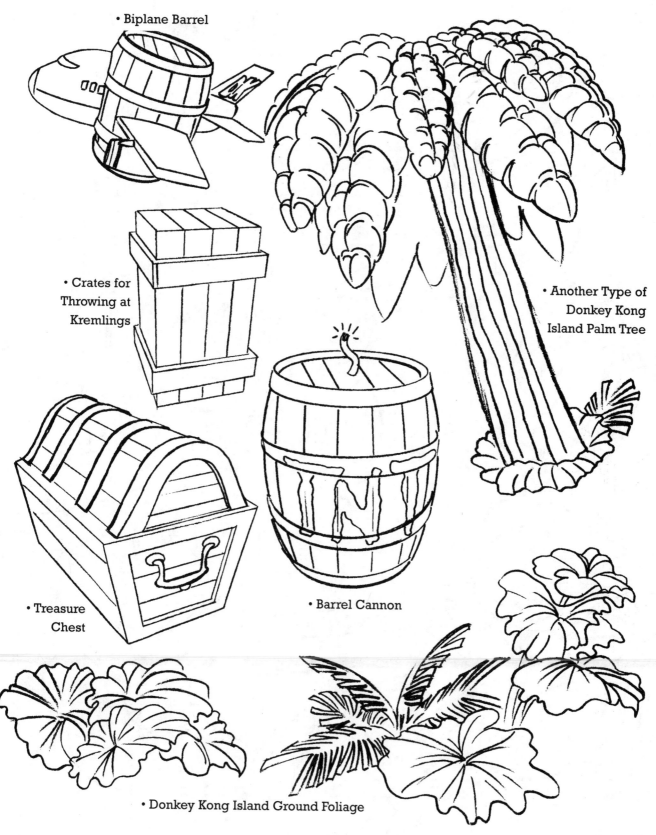

• Biplane Barrel

• Crates for Throwing at Kremlings

• Another Type of Donkey Kong Island Palm Tree

• Treasure Chest

• Barrel Cannon

• Donkey Kong Island Ground Foliage